THE BRAIN INJURY HANDBOOK

MEDICAL AND LEGAL PERSPECTIVES

SANDRA B. WORTHINGTON

PA PERSONAL INJURY ATTORNEY

WORTHINGTON LAW GROUP

Main Office: 1432 Bethlehem Pike, Flourtown, PA 19031

Telephone: 215-576-5150

email: sbw@WorthingtonLawGroup.com

www.WorthingtonLawGroup.com

Multiple satellite offices available to serve you in Center City Philadelphia and surrounding areas.

WORD ASSOCIATION PUBLISHERS

www.wordassociation.com

1.800.827.7903

Printed in the United States of America.

ISBN: 978-1-63385-242-6

Designed and published by

Word Association Publishers
205 Fifth Avenue
Tarentum, Pennsylvania 15084

www.wordassociation.com
1.800.827.7903

DISCLAIMER

While this book is meant to help people with brain injuries and their families to understand the medical side of brain injuries and the legal end of pursuing a claim, the contents of this book are neither legal nor medical advice. This book is purely intended to supplement other educational materials provided by your doctor and/or lawyer and to assist you in understanding brain injuries and legal claims revolving around brain injuries. Your receipt of the book from Worthington Law Group or anyone else does not create an attorney-client relationship between the firm or its lawyers and the individual reading this book. An attorney-client relationship cannot be formed in the absence of a written, signed, mutually acceptable, voluntary engagement agreement with a lawyer or law firm.

TABLE OF CONTENTS

Foreword 7

Acknowledgments 11

Chapter 1 - Basic Anatomy 15

Chapter 2 - Brain Injury - an Overview 23

Chapter 3 - Brain Injury Claims - The Legal Perspective . 37

Chapter 4 - Testimonials 49

Resources and Sources 63

FOREWORD

If you are reading this you or someone close to you has experienced a traumatic brain injury (TBI). This is a difficult and confusing time; hopefully this book will help.

A few years ago, I was hit by a car while in a crosswalk. The injuries were a damaged knee and a concussion. I remember trying to grab the windshield wiper as I hit the windshield and hood because I knew when the car stopped I would not. The next thing I remember, I was laying on the ground, trying to get to a sitting position and my eyes were telling me I was spinning. It took a while to get back to reality and recall what had just happened.

The knee was better in two months with just a brace and some rehab. It took me longer to recover from the concussion. For two months I had bad headaches that occurred at random. It was scary, but ibuprofen took care of most of it. For the next four months after that the headaches were less frequent and not as bad. However, the mere occurrence of these headaches and not knowing when they would happen was unsettling.

The worst result of the concussion was anosmia, a loss of the sense of smell. The headaches and knee pains were my primary concerns and it was a month before I realized that everything smelled the same. After more visits to the doctor, I learned it was a common result of a concussion and the sense might return in six months. Beyond six months of anosmia the chance was slim. So, there was more uncertainty about the future.

I feel rather lucky though as a loss of smell is rather minor compared to what could have happened. The accident happened in front of a store so I did get a video file of the event. The doctor said I was lucky, and after seeing my body bounce off the car and my head slam into the ground, I agreed.

Your injury might be less serious than mine or maybe more. Recovery and rehab is unique for every injury, but the common fact is it is scary, uncertain and expensive. Sometimes it is permanent and changes your life.

My advice to everyone is to learn as much as possible about the injury and your legal rights. Do not trust any one source and talk to several experts in every aspect.

The first lawyer I saw after the concussion was not very good. He rarely answered my calls, and when he did the common response was that he was still doing research. My comfort factor with him decreased with time until I finally decided to find another lawyer. This time I met with three lawyers, and that is how I met Sandra. She asked good questions, knew how to proceed and admitted when she did not have an answer. She did get back to me with those answers quickly and made sure I understood the result of all decisions. I felt more comfortable about the uncertainty of my recovery and future, and while she couldn't fix my injury, she cared about me. We worked together negotiating with the insurance companies, as every decision can have many results. This is Sandra's area of expertise and she shared her knowledge, so the future seemed a little less uncertain.

Years later when Sandra found articles about anosmia recovery therapy she sent them to me immediately. This is not something one expects from a lawyer, but it shows how much she cares about not just representing me on the legal side.

So please read this book and continue to learn about your injury and legal rights. Talk to lots of people and ask lots of questions. Your future will change because of the injury. Be positive and optimistic. Try to keep a sense of humor and enjoy what you have.

I may not be able to smell the roses anymore, but I also don't have to smell the stuff that makes them grow!

Randall Berwin,
Traumatic Brain Injury patient and
past client of Worthington Law Group

ACKNOWLEDGMENTS

I would like to express my profound appreciation to my friend, Douglas H. Baird, PhD, Director of the Pre-medical and Pre-health Division of the Graduate School of Biomedical Sciences and Professional Studies at the College of Medicine of Drexel University for his careful review and comments relating to the medical and anatomical portion of this book. It was of the utmost importance to me that the anatomical sections and descriptions as well as the legal portions, should be clear, accurate, and understandable to the layperson so that this guide might help a reader who is not a doctor or lawyer.

I also thank my long-term legal assistant, Marilyn Boyle, as well as my dear daughter, Rebecca, for proof-reading various drafts of this book countless times. Without their patience and tenacity, I doubt the book would have been published at all.

Finally, I would like to thank my client, Randy Berwin, for writing his heartfelt Foreword and for listening to me and following my advice so that I could get him the best possible result in his case. Representing such a client is not only an honor but makes the hard work involved in the practice of law worthwhile.

ABOUT SANDRA WORTHINGTON AND WORTHINGTON LAW GROUP:

Attorney Sandra Worthington has been practicing law for over 30 years, the majority of which have been devoted to fighting insurance companies and representing victims of accidents. She grew up in Montgomery County, Pennsylvania and attended the University of Virginia, graduating in 1978 with high distinction. She received her Juris Doctor degree at Temple University School of Law. Ms. Worthington worked for Crum and Forster Insurance Company in a management training program prior to attending law school, spending that time learning how insurance companies really work. She also worked for Weeks-Worthington Adjustment Company, a family owned independent insurance adjustment company servicing multiple large insurance companies in resolving auto accident and premises liability claims. Sandra Worthington has spent much of her professional life immersed in the insurance claims industry. She has seen both sides of these claims and knows just which tricks and tactics the insurance company will use to try to destroy your claim. Attorney Worthington was a partner with the law firm of Stocker and Worthington for over 20 years and was the founder of Worthington Law Group in 1998. Worthington Law Group is exclusively a personal injury law firm.

Ms. Worthington has handled countless traumatic brain injury cases, winning millions of dollars of awards and settlements for her clients. She is an avid fitness fanatic, was a Presidential Athlete and a National Champion Squash player who has been through four major joint surgeries and understands that getting back to a normal family life and the activities her clients love is critical to their existence.

Ms. Worthington is a member of the PA Bar Association, The PA Association for Justice, and has been rated as "Superb" by Avvo.com. She has been selected by Lawyers of Distinction as being in the top 10% of personal injury lawyers in the U.S. in 2017.

To read more about Attorney Worthington and the Worthington Law Group, go to www.WorthingtonLawGroup.com.

CHAPTER 1

BASIC ANATOMY

The Basics - What is the Brain?

The brain is a fascinating spongy, jelly-like organ made of nerve and supportive tissues. It is located in the bony covering we call the skull. The lower part of the brain is connected to the spinal cord. Together , the spinal cord and brain are known as the "central nervous system" or "CNS". The main job of the brain is to send "messages" to and control the body and organs.

How is the Brain Protected from Injury?

The combination of the skull, the meninges, cerebrospinal fluid, the blood-brain barrier and the skull all serve to protect the brain. The "meninges" is a membrane that covers and protects the brain and spinal cord. Cerebrospinal Fluid (CSF) cushions the spinal cord and brain. The brain is further protected by the blood-brain barrier which consists of flattened out cells tightly bound together which prevent blood-borne toxins from passing through. The brain is also obviously protected by the skull, which is bone.

Anatomy and Functions of the Brain:

The brain is one of the most complex and amazing organs in the human body. Although it weighs only about three pounds, the brain is the command center of the human body. The brain gives us awareness of ourselves and our surroundings, and processes a constant stream of sensory data. Each unique thought, feeling and plan for action is created by our brain. The brain controls muscular movement, the secretion of glands, our breathing and our internal temperature. It is important to understand the basic anatomy of the brain to understand brain injury. The diagrams below show the structure of the brain to help you visualize how certain types of trauma can interfere with the brain's ability to function.

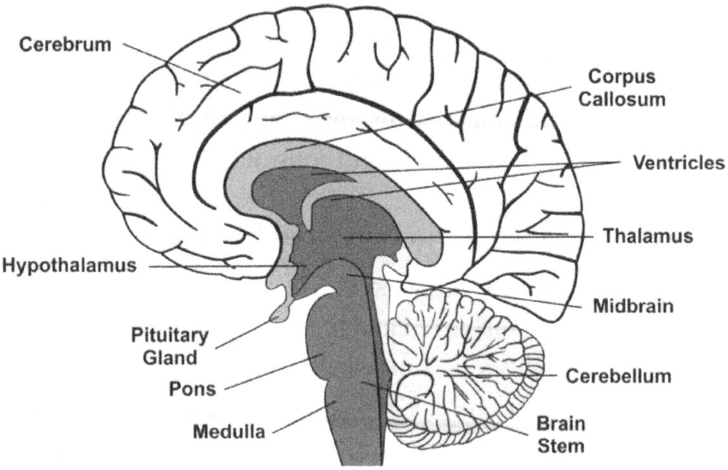

First of all, the brain is comprised of three main parts and thirty-two additional parts. The three main parts are:

1. ***The brainstem*** is located at the midline or middle of the brain and connects the brain to the spinal cord and controls automatic and basic survival functions such as breathing, sleep, digestion, heart rate and blood pressure, movement of the eyes and mouth. The brainstem relays sensory messages (hot, pain, loud, etc), hunger and involuntary

muscle movements such as sneezing, coughing, vomiting and swallowing. The function of the brainstem is so critical to our survival that injuries to it are often fatal;

2. ***The cerebellum***, located at the back of the brain which controls coordination and balance; and
3. ***The cerebrum***, covered by a wrinkly outer layer called the cortex, fills up most of the front of the skull and is involved in memory, problem solving, judgment, thinking and feeling, in addition to controlling voluntary movement.

The portion called the cerebrum is divided into four sections called "lobes". The cerebellum is located under the cerebrum. The purpose of the cerebellum is to coordinate muscular movement and to assist the body to maintain posture and balance. The cerebellum is attached to the brain stem. In essence, it controls the body's ability to balance by interpreting information sent to the brain by the eyes, ears and other sensory organs.

The cerebrum is the largest part of the human brain and is associated with higher brain function such as thought and action.

The four lobes of the brain located in the cerebrum are:

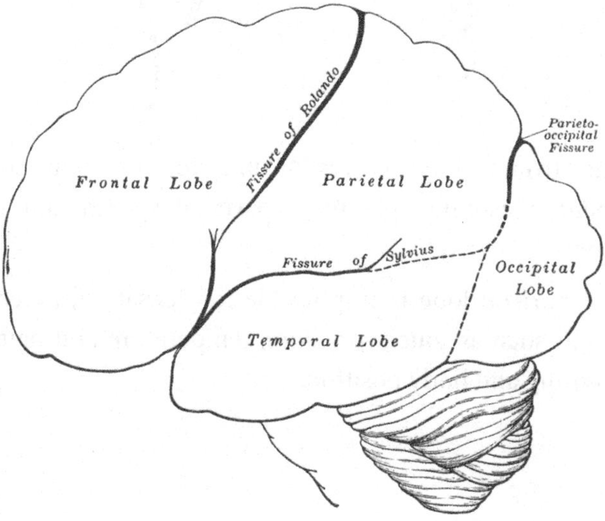

1. the frontal lobe
2. the parietal lobe
3. the occipital lobe
4. the temporal lobe

What is the Function of the Four Lobes?:

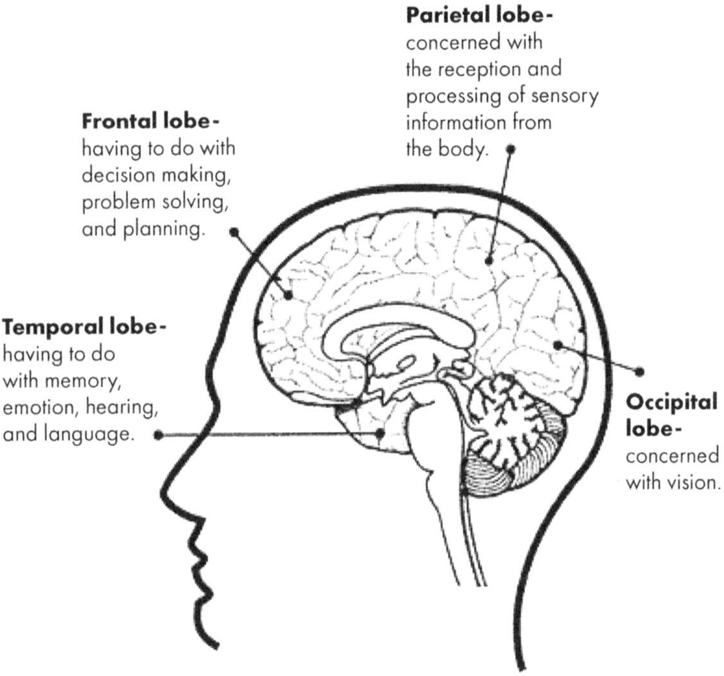

The frontal lobe is responsible for problem solving, judgment, reasoning, planning, parts of speech and motor function.

The parietal lobe is responsible for sensation, perception of stimuli such as touch, pressure, temperature and pain plus handwriting and body position.

The occipital lobe, located at the back of the brain behind the parietal and temporal lobe is concerned with many aspects of vision.

The temporal lobe is concerned with perception and recognition of auditory stimuli (hearing), aspects of language, and memory.

Left Brain-Right Brain Distinction:

The brain is divided into right and left halves.

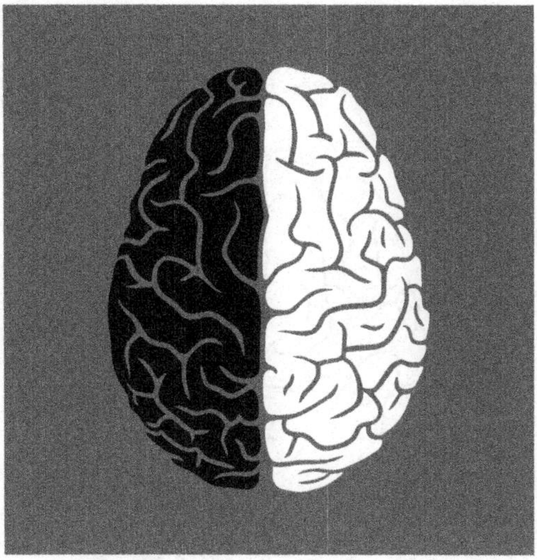

It is believed the two halves function differently, but experts are not completely certain how the "left brain" and "right brain" are distinguished in function, except it is fairly well accepted that:

1. The left half of the brain controls movement of the right side of the body, and,
2. The right half of the brain controls movement on the left side of the body

In most, but not all people, the language area is chiefly on the left. There is a popular though not completely accurate concept that people are "left-brained" or "right brained." One of these types is considered to be more literal, verbal and rigid while the other is considered more creative, impulsive and spatial. While this is not completely accurate, there is some inkling of truth to the concept that just as a person is left or right handed, a person does have a dominant hemisphere. Generally, the left is more involved in language while the right is usually more involved in spatial relations.

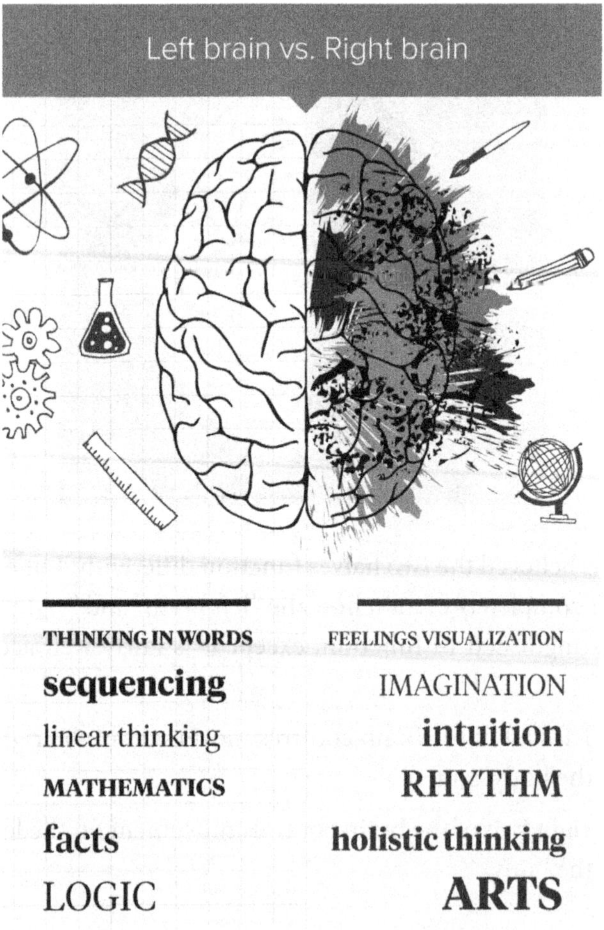

The "Neuron Forest":

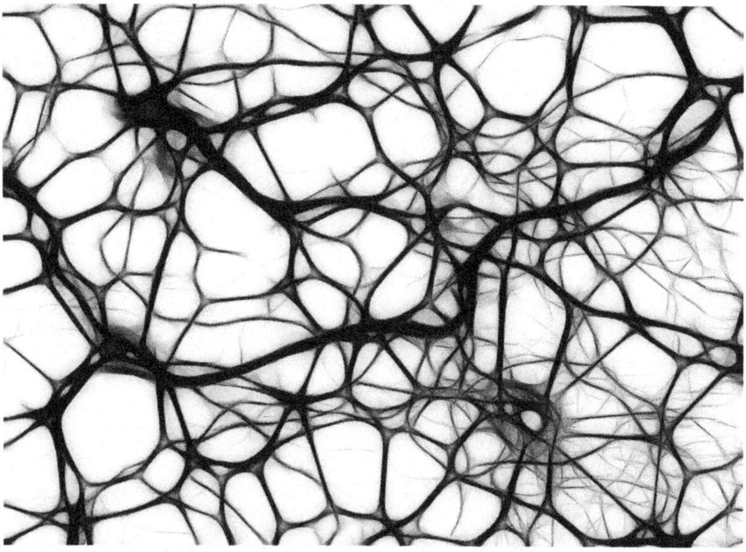

The true work of the brain occurs in the individual cells. The adult brain contains about one hundred BILLION nerve cells or neurons and has branches that connect at more than one TRILLION points! This dense, extensive branching network is known as the "neuron forest". The electrical signals moving through the neuron forest create the basis of feelings, memories and thoughts. It is widely believed that neurons are the main type of cell which is destroyed by Alzheimer's disease.

The signals that create memories and thoughts travel through an individual nerve cell as a tiny electrical charge. The nerve cells connect to each other at what are known as "synapses".

CHAPTER 2

BRAIN INJURY - AN OVERVIEW

How Does Traumatic Brain Injury Occur?

Traumatic brain injury can occur when an external mechanical force causes brain dysfunction. How does this happen? It usually results when there is a violent jolt or blow to the head or body. Obviously, an object actually penetrating the skull, such as a bullet or shattered piece of the actual skull can also cause traumatic brain injury. The location of the damage to the brain determines which functions and activities are affected.

Mild traumatic brain injury may cause temporary dysfunction of brain cells. More serious traumatic brain injury can cause bruising, torn tissues, bleeding and other physical damage to the brain which can result in long-term complications or even death.

What are the Symptoms of Traumatic Brain Injury?

Traumatic brain injury can have a vast array of physical and psychological effects. Some signs or symptoms can appear immediately after the traumatic event, while others may occur days or weeks after. The symptoms of mild TBI differ from those of moderate to severe TBI. How do they differ?

Mild Traumatic Brain Injury:

Symptoms of a mild traumatic brain injury can include:

*Headache

*Nausea/vomiting

*Temporary loss of consciousness

*No loss of consciousness, but a feeling of being in a stupor, dazed, fatigued, or drowsy

*Trouble sleeping

*Excessive sleeping (more than normal)

*Loss of balance or dizziness

*Sensory issues, such as ringing in the ears (tinnitus), a bad taste in the mouth or changes in the ability to smell

*Hypersensitivity to sound or light

*Memory issues or inability to concentrate as you did prior to injury

*Change in mood or personality

*Depression or anxiety

Moderate to Severe Brain Injuries:

Moderate to severe traumatic brain injuries can include the following symptoms, in addition to those from mild injuries listed above:

*Persistent headache that could worsen

*Multiple episodes of vomiting or nausea

*Loss of consciousness ranging from a few minutes to many hours

*Convulsions/seizures

*Pupil dilation in one or both eyes

*Clear liquid or fluids draining from the ears or nose

*Loss of coordination

*Severe confusion

*Combativeness or agitation

*Inability to wake up from sleep

*Coma or inability to recover consciousness

*Slurred speech

How Do These Symptoms Manifest Themselves in Children as Opposed to Adults?

It is critical to seek medical attention if either an adult or child has suffered a serious blow to the head, but in children, who cannot communicate as well as adults, one must pay particular attention to the following symptoms:

*Continual crying with inability to be consoled or unusual irritability

*Change in eating or nursing

*Sadness or depressed mood unlike prior to the injury

*Alteration of sleeping habits

*Loss of interest in typical activities or normally favored toy

The "Mechanics" of Brain Injury:

Now that you have a basic concept of the parts of the brain and how they work, you may wonder about the mechanics of how brain injury occurs. There are two fundamental ways that injury can occur. First, brain injury can occur when a relatively stationary head is struck by a moving object. For example, when a pedestrian standing at a bus stop is hit by the mirror on a passing truck. Second, brain injury can occur when a person's head and body are moving, as they are when one is a passenger in a car, and the car abruptly stops causing the passenger's head to catapult toward a stationary object such as the windshield or dashboard of the car. In both these situations, there is a huge amount of force and energy spontaneously transferred to the passenger's head and brain.

When either of these scenarios occur, the brain will move violently and will probably strike the inside wall of the skull. In this case, the cerebrospinal fluid surrounding the brain is often not sufficient enough to protect the brain from the force of the blow. Sometimes the brain will not only move forward and strike the front of the skull, but will rebound and strike the back of the skull afterward. This type of contact often results in what we call brain "contusions" which will occur in the areas of the brain closest to where the head hit the object. When the brain strikes the front of the skull, then deflects and hits the back of the skull, contusions can be formed on both the front and back of the brain. This type of injury has been named a "coup-contre-coup injury" which is a French term meaning "hit-opposite hit". It is a very common phenomenon.

What Types of Incidents Can Result in Brain Injury?

Many incidents can result in brain injury, although not all such incidents are the result of the negligence of another person or business. Brain Injuries can result from participation in sports, car and truck accidents, slips, trips and falls, items dropping on people from store shelves, construction accidents, ATV accidents, bicycle accidents, motorcycle accidents, pedestrian accidents, firearms accidents, defective products and incidents relating to explosions. Of course, there are all sorts of intentional acts, mostly criminal in nature, that can result in head injuries although we are not dealing with intentional acts (such as assault) in the legal section of this book. Similarly, we are not discussing military related head injuries although they are quite common, thus, have accelerated the study of closed head injuries. The list of potential causes of head injuries is seemingly endless.

The majority of the TBI cases we see in our office relate to various types of vehicular and pedestrian accidents, slips, trips and falls, construction accidents and heavy items falling from store shelves. In these cases, it is common for another individual or business to have negligently or recklessly caused the injury.

Causes of Falls in the Elderly Population:

The Centers for Disease Control (CDC) reports that in the U.S., over 35% of traumatic brain injuries are caused by falls, 17% are caused by motor vehicle accidents and 27% are caused by miscellaneous blows to the head. 21% of TBIs result from unknown causes while 10% result from assaults (a person striking another).

There are many reasons that brain injuries can result from falls and the older we get, the more likely this type of injury seems to be. Why? At least one-third of such falls among older folks involve hazards in the home such as unsafe stairs, lack or insufficiency of railings, poor lighting, throw rugs, electrical wires running across a floor, uneven ground and thresholds, broken concrete, slippery surfaces, incorrect use of canes or walkers. Medications such as tranquilizers, sedatives and antidepressants are big contributors to falls, as is alcohol. As we get older, balance and strength generally deteriorate, vision gets worse, muscle tone is diminished and gait is not as stable. Unfortunately, these issues are not normally addressed medically until AFTER the fall when physical therapy may be prescribed. However, I am a huge advocate of silver sneakers and elder fitness programs to prevent such problems from resulting in a fall. Sometimes a fall involves hitting the head which is never good, but in the case of the elderly or little children, can be particularly bad.

How Do Contusions Damage the Brain?

Contusions constitute injuries to the outer layer of the brain which you know from our introductory section is known as the "cortex" (grey matter). This grey matter consists of the tips of the brain cells. But, damage can also occur to the inside of the brain or axons which make up the white matter. Doctors often describe this type of injury as "diffuse axonal injury".

Contusions and diffuse axonal injury are common immediate trauma which can occur when someone hits their head during a car accident. Other consequences can also occur, such as bleeding inside the head and swelling of the brain. These symptoms often occur in delayed fashion and build with time after trauma and are a critical reason that head trauma needs to be immediately and closely monitored by medical staff since they can lead to a concussion (mild brain injury) or in the worst case scenario, a coma or death.

While the symptoms of mild brain injury in the form of a concussion will often improve substantially or even disappear without any long-term effects, a coma results from more severe brain trauma. A coma is a protracted state of unconsciousness and unresponsiveness.

How is the Severity of a Brain Injury Determined?

There is no way to accurately determine the length of time it will take for a TBI victim to recover. However, there are tests for measuring the severity of the brain injury. Generally, the severity of brain injury is measured by the following:

1. Glasgow Coma Scale:

What is the Glasgow Coma Scale? This scale measures the degree of responsiveness that the TBI patient exhibits immediately following the accident or, in the case of a coma, when the individual awakens. The scale, which has 15 points, involves administering a series of tests and a score is determined based on the victim's response to these tests. The tests involve assessments of eye movements, motor responses and verbal responses. The doctor will use this scale to measure responsiveness to verbal cues, pain, and orientation to surroundings. For example, if the TBI victim does not open his eyes when the doctor calls him by name, the score would be worse than if he opened his eyes immediately. The doctor will further determine whether the victim can speak at all and whether he can communicate, but does not understand what is happening. The victim's motor response is assessed based upon whether the victim can follow instructions to move body parts and whether they were unable to move at all or moved abnormally.

The Glasgow Coma Scale scores "grade" the TBI patient. For example, a score of 13-15 in a patient is generally considered to indicate a mild or minor brain injury. A score of 9-12 indicates a moderate injury. A score lower than 9 is indicative of serious brain injury.

2. Duration of Loss of consciousness:

Another method of measuring the severity of brain injury is based upon the length of time the victim is in a coma. Normally, the longer the coma, the more serious the head injury is determined to be, and therefore, the longer and less certainty for recovery from the injury. Note that simply opening one's eyes is not a definitive sign that one has come out of a coma. The patient must be able to actually follow simple commands as well to be considered out of the coma. Generally, a patient who has been in a coma for one hour or less is considered to have experienced a mild brain injury. Medical research indicates that a coma lasting six hours or more is a clear indication of severe brain injury.

3. Duration of Post-traumatic Amnesia (PTA):

The severity of a TBI may also be determined based upon the duration of time the victim's memory is significantly disturbed after the accident. This type of symptom is known as "post-traumatic amnesia," and manifests itself in confusion and disorientation, and significant inability to recall new information even though memory of old information is not flawed. Sometimes, the inability to recall new or very recent information will cause agitation and frustration in the patient. As a rule of thumb, doctors consider less than 24 hours of post-traumatic amnesia to be a sign of a mild or moderate brain injury, but anything longer is considered severe.

The Ranchos Los Amigos Scale:

This is another test utilized by medical staff to evaluate the severity of brain injury. This test is based upon cognitive and behavioral presentations as TBI victims emerge from a coma. The scale runs 1 through 8, with a grade of 1 signifying a person who is completely non-responsive and demonstrates no responsive cognitive functioning. A score of 8 demonstrates appropriate and purposeful functioning. TBI patients will progress up the scale as they recover, but recovery varies by the individual. Some patients plateau at a certain stage and do not progress, while others can make a full recovery. There are also many areas in between.

Neuropsychiatric Assessment:

Once it has been established the accident victim has suffered a potential TBI, a professional called a Neuropsychiatrist will sometimes be called in to evaluate the severity of the injury. The job of the Neuropsychiatrist is to root through the factors that influence how the brain is working in order to understand and explain abnormalities. The Neuropsychiatrist will perform tests to establish a comprehensive understanding of a patient's strengths and weaknesses. This is how the likely outcomes related to direct effects of brain injury can be determined and any difference between these and what is observed can be attributed to psychological reactions or independent events (not related to the head injury). Thus, in an individual who suffers from a severe psychotic condition that develops four months after a head injury with *no* loss of consciousness, it can be fairly accurately determined that the illness is not a direct result of the head trauma in regard to the formation of delusions. However, it is likely that the psychotic illness with delusions is indeed a direct effect of brain injury if the psychosis develops four months after a head injury in which the victim was in *a coma for two weeks* and suffered delirium for several more weeks.

Medicines for TBI:

Occasionally, the neuropsychiatrist, but not immediately after injury, will prescribe medications for the injury if the patient is experiencing severe or persistent agitation and/or aggression, mood issues such as depression, or seizures, but not always. Neuropsychiatrists must be very cautious in giving medications which may make things worse by causing confusion or other side effects. Certainly, the patient's family or caregivers should ask specific questions to understand the potential need for medications.

How Can Brain Injuries Be Treated And Rehabilitated?

A brain injury may require treatment and rehabilitation, sometimes on a long-term basis. Types of treatment which might be required are:

*Physical and occupational therapy

*Speech and language therapy to help the patient both understand and produce language as well as in how to organize daily tasks and develop problem solving methods

*Counseling to assist the patient in understanding their thoughts and to learn ways to cope with their feelings. This can help the patient to feel more in control and assist in getting back to normal life's activities

*Social support and support groups so that the patient gets a chance to talk with others going through the same issues. The patient's family and friends may be able to help them get treatment and deal with the symptoms

*Medicine to help relieve symptoms like sleep problems, chronic pain, headaches, anxiety, depression or memory issues.

Any or all of these may be helpful and should be discussed with the doctors involved in treatment. It is possible that the patient might have to try different types of treatment to determine which is or are most effective and help the patient to reduce symptoms, control emotions and resume enjoyment of life activities.

What Imaging is Best in Diagnosing a Traumatic Brain Injury?

The term Traumatic Brain Injury includes a variety of types of intracranial injuries which include not only the initial acute injury but also subsequent conditions which can occur after the initial acute injury. Standard x-rays of the head are not considered useful for diagnosis of the problems of the most concern after a traumatic brain injury as they only show bony abnormalities. Normally, in the ER, computed tomography (CT scan) is the first type of imaging that is used . The CT scan shows bone as well as tissue injuries, and is thus a better "one stop shop" to get to the root of major acute issues. Rarely is the MRI (magnetic resonance imaging) used at the ER for diagnostic purposes as it does not show issues with bone (ie, the skull). However, as the patient is followed after acute injury to monitor potential secondary issues which can develop such as cerebral herniation and swelling, the MRI becomes a useful tool and is more often used to perform follow up imaging. It is often said that 48-72 hours after an acute head injury the MRI is generally considered to be better than CT imaging.

Studies have revealed that less than 10% of patients considered to have experienced minor head injuries show positive findings on CT . The problem is distinguishing minor versus major head injuries which is often not an easy task. Some circumstances more clearly indicate a major injury than others. For example, worsening consciousness over time, loss of consciousness for more than 5 minutes, seizures, signs of penetrating skull injuries and other signs make it clear that imaging should be performed. Unfortunately, there is no foolproof test to be certain the imaging is necessary. And the imaging is very expensive and there are a limited number of CT machines to use at any given hospital ER. Therefore, the ER physician will often use other criteria to help decide whether imaging is indicated, such as the Glasgow coma scale, whether there is amnesia, vomiting and/or headache or other symptoms.

What Advances are Being Made in Diagnosing and Treating Brain Injuries?

There are many new cutting edge methods which are potentially going to be used in the future such as the neuro-optic tracking device called "EyeBOXCNS TM". By the time you read this, the EyeBOXCNS TM may be a common method of rapidly and accurately detecting brain abnormalities resulting from concussions and other head injuries by non-invasively measuring the effects of elevated intracranial pressure (ICP). Until now (2017), the sole way of accurately determining the level of intracranial pressure was by DRILLING A HOLE in the skull and placing a pressure-detecting probe directly in the brain to measure the ICP. Wow. Lots of people would not want to put themselves or their loved ones through that. I'm sure many people have died over the years from what were diagnosed as minor or moderate concussions but which resulted in ICP building up to lethal levels. The EyeBOXCNS TM is capable of diagnosing abnormal eye movement following brain injury but before symptoms appear. The EyeBOXCNS TM uses proprietary hardware and software to monitor eye movements while the patient watches a film clip for just under four minutes. Their eye movements correspond to specific neurologic functions to quantify the physiologic impact of ICP. The reason this is important is that continued intracranial pressure is believed to be the cause of some of the sudden deaths that occur when sports players go back into the game with a concussion and suffer a second blow to the head. This condition is called "second impact syndrome". The company that developed this test, Oculogica, Inc. is awaiting FDA clearance for this device. If it passes the test, the EyeBOXCNS TM would be the first neuro-optic tracking device approved by the FDA to diagnose concussions and other traumatic brain injuries.

This and other devices will no doubt be invented for more and more precise, less invasive methods of diagnosing the severity of ICP and TBI.

Also being tested currently are new technologies such as transcranial magnetic stimulation (TMS) which basically uses repetitive magnetic pulses to improve specific symptoms. This therapy, if approved, may potentially help with issues like depression associated with TBI and perhaps other symptoms. By the time you read this, many additional new technologies will probably be in the process of testing or use.

A wonderful breakthrough in February 2018 as reported by the American Psychiatric Association, was the approval by the FDA of a blood test, developed by Banyan Biomarkers, which is capable of diagnosing mild TBI or concussion. The blood test is called the Brain Trauma Indicator and works by measuring levels of two proteins that are released from the brain following a head injury and appear in the blood within hours of the injury. Previous to this test being available, a doctor basically had no alternative to using the 15-point Glascow Coma Scale followed by ordering a CT scan for a head injury patient in the ER. A CT scan exposes the patient to substantial radiation. In addition, more than 90% of patients presenting to the ER with mild TBI or concussion have a negative CT scan. The Brain Trauma Indicator test can reliably predict the absence of intracranial lesions which will allow a doctor to rule out the need for an expensive CT scan in at least one-third of patients, plus save that patient exposure to unnecessary radiation. When you consider that according to the US Centers for Disease Control and Prevention, there were estimated to be 2.8 MILLION incidents involving TBI ER visits, this is a breathtaking development!

A CT scan can range in price from $800-$1500 (as of the writing of this book). The current version of the blood test will cost approximately $150 and can be taken within 12 hours of injury. The results can be obtained within three or four hours. No doubt the test will be tweaked and improved by scientists over time which will make a diagnosis of mild traumatic brain injury far easier, faster, less expensive and less dangerous to the patient.

It is not known how this blood test can determine subconcussive or repeated hits which are hits that don't cause symptoms but do cause brain injury. This type of injury can result from certain collision and contact sports. Repeated hits to the head are thought to be the root of the neurodegenerative disease called chronic traumatic encephalopathy, or CTE which I discussed in regard to the NFL lawsuit mentioned in this book. The good news is that Banyan Biomarkers is partnering with another company called Quanterix to develop a method to combine the biomarkers of Banyan with digital technology that can look at the proteins at a super microscopic level and pinpoint low level concentrations of the proteins. The goal is to further refine testing methods to improve sensitivity in order to enable better diagnosis, better brain health and to assist in finding ways to protect athletes, soldiers and others subjected to repeated hits.

There are many organizations involved in research and study of traumatic brain injury and we can only hope they continue to find new and non-invasive methods to diagnose and treat TBI.

Who Can You Contact to Read More About Traumatic Head Injuries?

Of course, there is a lot of research going on regarding diagnosis and treatment of head injuries. Which organizations can be contacted for more information? A good starting point is The Brain Association of America (www.biausa.org). This site has no end of resources.

CHAPTER 3

BRAIN INJURY CLAIMS - THE LEGAL PERSPECTIVE

Why am I Discussing These Scales and Tests?

The reason I am discussing these scales and diagnostic methods is not only so that you understand what they mean if the doctor has not explained them to you, but also to help you understand how they impact a legal case involving traumatic brain injury. When I am trying to determine whether a TBI victim has a valid and provable case, the more objective data I have to evaluate the level of injury, the better I can present the case in court. By reviewing medical evidence from licensed medical doctors, brain scans, and objective testing I can determine whether it will be possible to prove in court that my client has a traumatic brain injury.

Does the Client Have a Case I Can Prove and Win?

All of this is the foundation of explaining to you what I and other lawyers need to be able to prove and win a traumatic brain injury case. Think of it this way -- if my client breaks his leg in a rear-ender car accident in which he is struck from behind, the injury and fault are clear. If all cases were so simple, people would not need lawyers to represent them. The difficulty in my job comes when an injury is not immediately clear and apparent or fault for the accident is not obvious. To proceed to represent any injured person in an accident claim, I need to prove the defendant was, indeed, negligent. I need to prove that the defendant was at fault for my client's injuries due to his negligence. And, I need to prove the negligence caused the injury. How can I do that when the injury is largely invisible? It isn't easy!

If I can establish that the defendant was negligent and caused my client's injury, then I can use medical records and testimony of doctors in court to prove this often invisible but severe type of injury. It is not enough for the client to sit and testify he hit his head or hasn't been able to think clearly since the accident. Often there is no visible evidence that the victim has actually hit his head. In fact, a concussion can be caused without any head impact. However, If the windshield has a spider-web shaped crack on it after the accident and there is a cut or bruise on my client's forehead, that is certainly a good start. But, even that doesn't prove how BAD the injury is. That is where the scales and scans come in. If I can prove the impact and the Glasgow scale is measured by the doctor at an 8, I have convincing, objective evidence of a serious brain injury. The bottom line is that the only thing that matters once a lawsuit is filed is the evidence that can actually be proved in court. Subjective descriptions of memory loss by the TBI patient and the family can be persuasive, but not so much if the objective evidence does not support the victim's testimony. I must be able to explain and demonstrate how the accident probably did cause a head injury.

Negligence and Causation - You Need Both of These to Prove Your Case:

If we know from our objective and subjective evidence that the victim has, indeed, suffered a brain injury, and we have proved that someone else was negligent (i.e., was texting and rear-ended my client's car), now my job is to prove that the negligence CAUSED the head injury. For example, what if my client was skiing the week prior to the accident and had a documented fall for which he was in the hospital. How can I prove that the head injury was caused by the car accident and not a residual injury from the skiing accident? And don't think that scenario has not occurred because I have seen it! Well, I could compare the ER testing from the skiing accident to the ER testing from the car accident. If I can show that the Glasgow scale was a 12 after the ski accident, but was a 3 after the car accident, *that* is persuasive, although the case would still not be a "slam-dunk" winner. Perhaps the first head injury contributed to the severity of the second. So as you can see, it is complicated! All that matters is what I can PROVE. I have to prove that not only was the defendant negligent, but that the negligent act CAUSED the injury. Even if I believe you 100%, if I cannot prove the case with **admissible evidence** and testimony, I cannot file suit.

The Truth is the Truth Everywhere, Right?

No. The truth as you know it outside the courtroom is different than the truth INSIDE the courtroom (as well as inside the adjuster's head). The truth inside the courtroom is all that matters to me as a lawyer. The truth inside the courtroom is what I can PROVE by evidence. It doesn't matter that I believe you 100%. If I do not think I can win your case with actual evidence, I cannot accept your case. This may sound awful to you, but it is true and any good lawyer with a lot of experience will tell you the same thing. I am not writing this book to tell you what you want to hear, but what you need to know.

Consider the recent case by the NFL in which it agreed to settle for $765 million dollars with retired NFL players who claimed to have suffered brain injuries during their professional football careers. The principal allegation by the players was that the NFL had knowledge that years of head impacts in the players' careers could lead to serious damage to the brain. The NFL had scores of scientists studying this in the players. Sadly, many of the brain injuries could not be properly identified until the autopsy and examination of the brain of certain deceased players.

Unfortunately, a person in a car accident does not have the benefit of a consortium of world renowned scientists and doctors to prove that the victim suffered a serious or permanent brain injury. Each case is different. Sometimes the accident victim's doctor will not see him until weeks after the injury rather than in the ER immediately following trauma. The signs of what caused the injury may not be anywhere near as obvious as immediately after the injury. Unless an independent witness actually saw the victim hit his head (which is rare), if the victim was stunned, he may not even know he hit his head. Or perhaps he didn't hit his head, but was severely jolted while strapped into a seat belt allowing the momentum and force of the accident to cause the brain to bounce back and forth off of the interior of the skull, but with no evidence of physical contact. These are very difficult cases which are not always possible to win. We are forced to turn down some cases like this because we cannot establish the truth in the courtroom to a jury or judge. This is one very good reason to go to the ER immediately after an accident instead of waiting three weeks to see if your dizziness or memory loss dissipate. Those objective tests I was talking about would have been performed and helped me to prove the TBI.

What Kinds of Head Trauma Cases Have I Handled?

I have handled many kinds of traumatic brain injury cases ranging from mild concussion to severe, life-altering head injuries. In some of these cases, the victim has been able to make a good recovery over time, although the risk of another head injury making matters worse is always looming over these victims. I have handled head injuries in which someone has permanently lost the ability to smell (anosmia) and in which the victim has developed double vision in one eye. Think about how those types of injuries might affect your life. I have handled some TBI cases in which due to a bike accident the victim developed amnesia which lasted for over six months. I have represented head injury victims who were in a coma for a full week or more before, thankfully, regaining consciousness with miraculously few residual consequences. Unfortunately, I have also represented victims and their families after a head injury has caused death. Each case is different and the continuum of effects on the victim's life can vary in infinite ways, all of which need to be considered carefully and presented clearly.

Often, the family doctor will not notice the consequences of the head injury in the days or weeks following a head injury and it is the client's family or lawyer who notices changes in behavior. If you think about it, most doctor appointments are fairly short in duration. Many times, although you may wait a half hour or more for your appointment, you may only be in with your primary doctor for fifteen minutes or less. If there are subtle personality changes, depression or forgetfulness, even the family doctor may not notice, especially if the victim is unaware he is experiencing residual brain injury. I have had family members call and tell me their loved one has been forgetting appointments, job interviews, or where he put the keys. At first all of that may seem like mere distraction or perhaps age-related memory loss. But, the persistence and extremity of such symptoms may only be noticed by a family member seeing it day in and day out.

As the lawyer for brain injured clients, I have noticed changes in personality in some of them. I had one client who repeatedly promised to take steps I had requested related to his case. He completely forgot on two occasions to take these important steps which we discussed in detail. He also forgot that I had told him! I knew something was wrong, but this individual lived alone and was not working at the time of the accident. There were no local family members or co-workers to point out his behavior to him. I pointed it out to make sure he was fully evaluated. I was the only person speaking to him on a regular basis and thus I was the only person aware of the problem. He was thankfully evaluated and treated then made a very good recovery. However, we never could have proved the seriousness of the head injury if I had not had regular contact with him and pointed out he was having serious memory issues that warranted testing and treating.

How To Choose a Lawyer For Your Brain Injury Claim:

Many times, victims of brain injuries resulting from motor vehicle crashes, pedestrian injuries, falls, defective products or other negligence find it beneficial to consult with an attorney who has experience in personal injury cases involving brain injury. In light of the expensive and often extensive requirement for medical, rehabilitation and long-term care that the brain injured person and his family face, all potential financial resources need to be investigated vigorously. Besides the injury case itself, legal issues can arise relating to competency/guardianship, eligibility for disability or other federal or state entitlement programs, estate planning, powers of attorney, separation and divorce and criminal matters. Your lawyer should be able to guide and direct you to experts in those fields to ensure your needs are being anticipated and met.

The legal system may afford the person whose brain injury resulted from the negligence or recklessness of others with the resources necessary to maximize financial recovery as well as to provide for long-term care and support needs. Tort law, which applies in personal injury cases is intended to encourage safety and discourage negligent or reckless acts which cause injury. The objective is to obtain full and fair compensation for pain and suffering and loss of enjoyment of life as well as payment of past and future lost wages (loss of earning potential) and past and future medical and rehabilitation bills, related to the brain injury.

When Should You Seek the Advice of an Attorney After a Brain Injury?

You should seek legal advice as soon as possible after the injury. Important evidence can be lost if an attorney is not involved early on in the process following the injury. The attorney can be performing important investigative work while you are focusing on care for the injured victim.

Many people tell me they cannot afford a lawyer, but in a case like this, there is no payment to the attorney unless he or she wins the case. In addition, the attorney advances all costs of the case and you do not have to pay them back unless the case is won. At that point, and depending upon the fee agreement you have with the lawyer, you would pay back the costs only if the lawyer is victorious in court or settles the case.

How Do you Figure Out Who the Defendant (Negligent Party) is?

Another critical reason to get an experienced lawyer on board quickly is that it is not always easy to determine exactly who was responsible for the injury. In the case of a DUI driver hitting a pedestrian victim on the street in a crosswalk, not only would the driver be a defendant, but potentially the bar that served him alcohol to the point of intoxication. Perhaps the stop sign was missing for six months and had not been replaced at the crosswalk. Then you might have the state or local government as a potential defendant as well. It is up to the attorney to identify any and all potentially liable defendants and it isn't always easy to do. The more quickly the lawyer can jump on the investigation, the more likely it will be that you will locate and identify the responsible parties.

You will see no end of advertisements on television for lawyers if you are stuck at home rehabilitating. Many of them are offensive. Many say the same things over and over and over. They involve aggressive lawyers, paying the TV station to "toot their own horns" about how big and mean and aggressive they are. But, do they really have the credentials to win your case? And, will you actually like to work with (and trust) an attorney based on a TV ad? Very possibly not. You want a lawyer with extensive experience and accomplishments. You want it to be someone you do not dread calling and not someone whom you can never reach because his office is like a conveyor belt of injury cases. You don't want to hire the lawyer in the ad then be passed off to an associate with 5 years of experience or to a paralegal.

Choosing a lawyer to represent you in any type of legal case is much like choosing your family doctor or your heart surgeon.

You don't want to sit and tell your medical troubles to someone who doesn't care about you or who doesn't have the experience to do your surgery. Mostly, people ask friends for referrals to such professionals, but now you can also look at ratings on the internet for all kinds of professionals. You can also read what their own patients or clients say about them. In fact, on Avvo.com you can find a lawyer in your geographic area and read not only what their past clients have said about them, good or bad, but also what other LAWYERS say about them. In addition, most lawyers have a website you can review to get a feel for their approach to cases and their level of experience.

Look into the education and training of the lawyer, extent of legal experience, knowledge of the consequences and treatment of brain injury, knowledge of how to structure and manage awards, and experience with similar cases. Also, you should LIKE your lawyer – he or she will be a critical part of your life for what may be years while your case goes to court or while your injured loved one goes through lengthy rehabilitation or surgery.

Note that the attorney has an important decision to make also. Attorneys invest a substantial amount of time, energy and money to investigate, prepare and resolve a case at their own expense and without a dime from the client (unless they win). Imagine working for two or three years without compensation. In a contingent fee arrangement which is the typical method of payment, the attorney does not get one red cent if he or she doesn't win the case. As a result of the tremendous financial risk involved, attorneys may decline a case if they do not believe there is a good chance of success or if it is determined that the defendant has no insurance or no assets.

I hope this small book has given you a lot of useful information regarding traumatic brain injury and TBI claims and lawsuits. If you or your loved one was injured in an accident resulting in a TBI, I certainly hope this book helps to inform you and to guide you regarding the medical treatment and the legal aspects of the situation.

What Critical Steps Should I Take in Pursuing a Claim for a Brain Injury Aside from Choosing the Right Lawyer?

First: It is important that you take photos of what you believe to be the cause of the brain injury. For example, if you tripped on a broken step make sure you or someone you know takes several photos of the step showing the defect. Such photos are even more useful if there is a ruler or measuring tape showing the height and width of the stairs. If you struck your head on the windshield and there is a spider-web type crack, take a photo of it because once the car is repaired or totaled you won' t have access to that critical evidence anymore. If you slipped on dark liquid in a mall, take a photo of the liquid as well as any soda dispenser nearby or any empty cup that might be lying nearby on the floor on its side. You get the idea -- you need as much proof as is possible and photos are an unsurpassed way to accomplish this goal.

Second: If the insurance company for the responsible party calls you or arrives at your home to speak to you DON'T DO IT. They may try to bully you or frighten you into giving a statement. Tell them in no uncertain terms that you will not give a statement, but you will accept their business card. Then hire an experienced personal injury lawyer and hand the card to him or her.

Third: Attend all medical appointments and seek all recommended treatment. Make sure you tell your doctor all your symptoms. If you believe you have suffered a head injury take a relative with you who can enlighten the doctors about your behavior. You may not realize you are forgetting things, but your spouse or closest relative certainly knows this. If your doctor wants you to go to have a brain scan, do it as soon as possible.

Fourth: DO NOT WRITE ABOUT YOUR ACCIDENT OR INJURIES ON SOCIAL MEDIA or discuss your injuries with friends in person. Do not post photos of yourself or anyone in the accident.

Fifth: Do not discuss the legal end of your case with your doctor. Stick to your medical issues. Some doctors do not like lawyers and most do not have any interest in getting involved in a legal claim or lawsuit. Do not mention your case or your lawyer to your doctor -- just get whatever treatment you need and leave the legal stuff to the lawyer. At the end of your treatment, or before, your lawyer will order all records and bills necessary to pursue the claim.

Sixth: If your doctor has told you to stay out of work due to your brain injury, you MUST get a **disability note** from the doctor stating which date you became disabled from work and when he thinks you will return. He can always extend that date if you are not ready to return, but you will need a note extending the time frame to another date. If you do not do this, even if you are out of work for three months your employer's records will simply reflect that you took "sick days" or "personal days". Your lawyer will not be able to get you reimbursed for those days unless your employer has the disability note stating the reason for your absence and the exact time frame.

CHAPTER 4

TESTIMONIALS

(RATED 5.0 OUT OF 5.0 STARS)

What Our Clients Say About Us:

Here is what our clients have written about us on Avvo.com, Google and elsewhere:

"Your expertise, competency and time spent on my case along with honest straightforward answers to my questions made me feel comfortable and confident in your abilities. Your prompt, personal responses to my calls and letters showed a high level of commitment and concern for my best interests.

Your outstanding professional attitude, high level of integrity and just as importantly, your caring manner, made me feel respected as a person and not merely as a client."

-Mrs. Nancy A.

"After my accident, I had so much to worry about: I was attempting to nurse my wounds and get my life back in order. Thank goodness I never had to worry about how my case was being handled. You never failed to keep me informed or answer any of my questions."

"The results that you and your staff obtained for me were more than I had expected or even thought possible."—

-Anthony L.

Sandra Worthington is one of the best attorneys I have ever had the pleasure of working with. She was extremely helpful from the very beginning and handled my case with the highest professionalism throughout. The Worthington Law Group is an honest, dedicated team you would always want on your side. I highly recommend Sandra and will always look to her for any help I may need in the future.

-H. Naseer, Montgomery County, PA

The Worthington Law Group helped me through a difficult time and I am extremely grateful for their help. Sandra Worthington always went above and beyond when helping me with my case. I strongly recommend this law group for anyone who is suffering from an accident!

-S. Veneziale, Bucks County, PA

I am lucky I found Sandra. The best attorney I have ever worked with.

Sandra represented me in a case where I was involved in a car accident caused by a drunk driver. I called a few attorneys and quickly settled on Sandra to assist me. She immediately started an organized effort to get my case moving forward, advising me every step of the way on what to expect and what I needed to be doing. There were no surprises. She is amazing in her knowledge of the law and victims' rights. I will be recommending her to any family and friends that have a need for a fantastic attorney.

-5.0 stars - Posted by Troy - December 2, 2016

On Top of Her Game!

I was introduced to Sandra B. Worthington about six years ago through an attorney friend of mine. I knew she specialized in personal injury law, but never thought I would need her services.

Three years ago I was hit by a DUI motorist in a head-on collision. I retained the services of Ms. Worthington. Even though this motor vehicle accident complicated my life, Ms. Worthington's experience in personal injury law made things much easier for me in handling this matter. She was in touch with me often and was always available to listen and answer my questions. She walked me through the case, step by step, and in the end, she won my case! I was very pleased with the outcome.

If you have any doubt as to whether you have a case or not, Ms. Worthington will steer you in the right direction. She is no nonsense and will tell you the truth!

I highly recommend Ms. Worthington. She is on top of her game in the field of personal injury law.

-5.0 stars - Posted by anonymous - February 12, 2011

"I have and will continue to recommend you to others. Your outstanding professional attitude, high level of integrity and caring manner made me feel respected as a person and not merely as a client."

-Mrs. N.A. of Bucks County, PA

I surely would recommend!

Sandra was there for me every step of the way with my case. She was always there to listen and available when needed. I was very happy to have her by my side throughout the entire process. She made me feel like I didn't have to worry about anything. I would highly recommend Sandra because she was very helpful in getting my case resolved with the utmost care.

-5.0 stars - Posted by T. Morton - July 27, 2016

Prompt and Efficient.

Sandra was extremely time-efficient and cooperative throughout the whole process. I never had any doubt that she would resolve the case, and I definitely felt that I was in good hands. I would recommend her first to anyone in need of an attorney.

-5.0 stars - Posted by Rafi - May 25, 2017

Dedicated and Professional.

Sandra was always quick to reply to emails from day one. She provided me with not only her opinion, but also explained a lot of complicated law processes that were going on throughout my case. She wanted me to stay informed. She was very organized and made the case on my end pretty effortless. I enjoyed how often Sandra used her intellect to invest the best arguments for my case. I often felt like she was not only working hard for me, but she also cared. Investigators and photographers were just all brought straight to me. It was a great experience and the end result was not only a won case, but also a great professional relationship. Hiring Sandra is the first step to succeeding in your case.

-5.0 stars - Posted by anonymous - May 19, 2016

Honest.

I so appreciate Sandra Worthington. She gave me the best advice about my car accident that I was involved in over 2 years ago. Being confused and frustrated about this accident was the worst thing for me. She gave me great advice and other contact information to get in touch with people I needed to speak with. If you need a lawyer to represent you call Sandra Worthington. She is very knowledgeable about her brand in law. Thanks again Sandra. You were very much appreciated.

-5.0 stars - Posted by Tiffiny - May 11, 2016

Hope I never need her again but glad I used her.

Sandra handled my case efficiently, kept me in the information loop and addressed any concerns I had. She researched the injury, determined appropriate compensation and negotiated settlement in a very timely manner. She went beyond my expectations and made excellent suggestions regarding my therapy and recovery process. I would recommend her without hesitation.

-5.0 stars - Posted by anonymous - August 20, 2015

Amazing Lawyer.

Sandra has been amazing throughout this whole journey with my case. She has been a great lawyer and a friend. She's loyal, confident, and honest. She did everything she could to get what I deserved. I recommend her to anyone that needs a lawyer. She's one of the best!

-5.0 stars - Posted by Agron - June 16, 2015

Involved in a Traffic Accident: Researched Lawyers and Found Sandra.

Having never been involved in a lawsuit, I had no idea what to expect, what not to expect, and most of all, what Sandra taught me about the law. When I called Sandra and explained to her what had happened, she was comforting and more than willing to address my concerns in regards to the accident. The initial telephone interview put me at ease and after we met in person, I felt secure that I had found the perfect lawyer. I never once doubted her knowledge nor her expertise. If I had a question, and did not understand specifics, she explained the legal terms in layman's terms. I was very satisfied with the monetary amount at the conclusion of my case. If I am in need of a lawyer in the future, I would not hesitate for a moment to call Sandra. With that said, I would most definitely refer Sandra to anyone who needs an outstanding lawyer.

-5.0 stars - Posted by anonymous - March 20, 2015

Simply, the best!

Sandy Worthington has been my Attorney for over 20 years. She has been successful in every instance that I needed her help, which has been more times than I ever imagined it would be.

The first time I met her was during my divorce and child custody case in the early 1990's. I believe that was the last divorce she handled so please don't contact her for that, although I am certain she would recommend someone good to anyone who asked. During that time we had 3 mediation hearings for support and custody of my son. She was 3 for 3, our side winning every time. Back then, as it is even today, a Dad usually is at a disadvantage during a child custody case.

A few years later I remarried and my wife was killed in a traffic accident. On that terrible morning, after I spoke to my wife's daughter, Sandy was the next phone call I made. That is how high I value her guidance, advice and knowledge. Even though she had nothing to do with the D.A.'s case against the woman charged with killing my wife, Sandy came to the Courthouse every day to be with me as we watched the trial. Sandy must have heard something that a lot of people missed. After the trial concluded, Sandy recommended that we hire an Accident Reconstruction Specialist to find out what really happened. She discovered the facts that caused the accident and she went after the people and company that was responsible. Once again, at every opportunity, she made the right moves and was successful in our negotiations. Over that time, I probably spoke to her hundreds of times in person and on the phone.

Every single time we talked I know more, felt better and had a greater understanding of what was going on in the process.

Probably the highest compliment I can pay to her, is whenever I hear people speaking about an attorney or their attorney, it's not always in a positive manner. In those instances I always say, "you must have the wrong attorney. I love my Attorney. Her name is Sandy Worthington and you need to call her."

-5.0 stars - Posted by Matthew - March 10, 2015

Took the time to not only advise, but teach and empower me!

In the middle of an insurance nightmare where I was getting bullied into an unfavorable settlement that would have dangerously limited my rights, I called Sandra (among several other lawyers) to see if I needed representation. Of all the people I spoke with, Sandra was the only one to speak to me as a person and not a dollar sign. She didn't even flinch when I said I didn't necessarily want to pursue a lawsuit, just that I wanted to know my options. She took the time to not only explain everything to me in full detail (answering questions I didn't even know I had), but to empower me as an individual. Oh, and did I forget to mention -- she did this without asking for a dime or pushing me to hire her. I don't know many lawyers who would take the time to do that.

-5.0 stars - Posted by Kimberly - September 5, 2014

Sandra Worthington finds justice for my injured sons

A number of years ago when my two sons were in their early teens we were involved in an automobile accident on our way to a local ski area. Another vehicle ran a stop sign right in front of us directly into our path, and I was unable to avoid a collision. I can still remember the surprise registered on the driver's face as he pressed on his brake pedal to no avail. Both boys were injured; I was unharmed.

After a number of unsuccessful attempts to get either the manufacturer or the garage where the other driver had taken his vehicle for brake repairs to accept responsibility for the brake failure, I called Sandra. She was able to obtain a rapid, out-of-court settlement that was very fair. Further, she had the money put into CD's that matured into sizable amounts for their college educations.

I was and remain deeply impressed by Sandra's intelligence, professionalism and efficiency. I recommend her highly.

-5.0 stars - Posted by Julian - March 13, 2014

Tenacious in her quest for success in clients cases!

I was involved in an accident several years ago and first met Sandy at that time, unfortunately I did not realize that I did not have the correct amount of insurance to protect myself at that time and after my consultation with Sandy where she let me know what the correct levels are I quickly corrected that with my agent the very next day. Had it not been for that consultation with Sandy I would not have been protected this time when I was struck from behind by an inattentive driver that sent myself and my wife into physical therapy for a few months. Thanks to Sandy for caring enough back when I wasn't covered properly to make sure I was covered this time -- I always recommend Sandy to all my friends, family, coworkers and if asked who I would recommend, my customers - I happen to work for a body shop in the tri-state area.

-5.0 stars - Posted by anonymous - December 18, 2013

A client reviews attorney Sandra B. Worthington

While on the job as a courier for a large delivery company I was bitten by a customer's small dog. I contacted attorney Sandra Worthington and told her what had happened to me, etc. She spoke to me in a very kind and respectful manner. Sandra took my case and within a few short months won for me a nice monetary settlement. My case was very small, but she treated me like I was a big time client! I highly recommend attorney Sandra Worthington! She cares about her clients!

-5.0 stars - Posted by Paul - November 3, 2013

I would like to share my families experience with Sandra Worthington, Attorney At Law.

We have used Ms. Worthington for 2 cases in the last several years. Both have had good outcomes and we were very pleased with her work. She is very attentive to her client's needs, she returns calls and emails very promptly and keeps her clients informed up to the minute with latest developments. She is also very good about listening to what you have to say and not interrupting, but also advising in a very knowledgeable way. There hasn't been a question that I have asked of her that she didn't know the answer to and isn't afraid to tell the truth which is one of the things that is very hard to find. I wouldn't hesitate to call her again in the future should the need come or to pass along her name and number to a friend or family member. One last thing, her office staff is very nice to deal with and very helpful.

-5.0 stars - Posted by anonymous - June 21, 2013

Excellent representation

Sandra won a difficult accident case for me. During the entire process she kept me informed and made sure all my questions were answered. She promptly returned my emails and phone calls. I would not hesitate to ask for her help again or recommend her to others.

-5.0 stars - Posted by Cheryl - March 23, 2013

Determined

Sandra did a wonderful job representing me. I had a pre-existing condition that was worsened by my accident. Sandra made sure that I was treated and compensated fairly. Would definitely recommend Sandra, she is an excellent attorney.

-5.0 stars - Posted by Florence - August 24, 2012

Outstanding Legal Representation

The first time I talked with Sandy Worthington I felt completely at ease. She had experience and was knowledgeable of the Pennsylvania dog bite law regarding my type of case. Over the next few years she guided me through a maze of legal and medical issues relating to the injury I had received. During these years a mutual respect based on honesty and clear communication grew between Sandy and I, and that respect continues to this day. Sandy did an incredible job representing me, being clear about what she was doing keeping me informed along the way, taking the time to be thorough and truly careful about the legalities of my case. Most importantly she was considerate and thoughtful and truly cared about me as a person, I did not feel like "just another client." Choosing Sandy Worthington to represent me during such a traumatic time in my life was the smartest step I could have taken and I am certainly glad I did!

-5.0 stars - Posted by Nancy - August 10, 2012

Awesome Attorney!

I have had quite a few experiences with Sandra, whether it was over a case that she was hired for or just questions that I had. Sandra was very prompt in responding to me, each and every time and extremely helpful. She did everything she could to make the experience of a legal case, as pleasant, easy and as hassle-free as possible. I could call Sandra at anytime with any issue and if it was not an area of Sandra's expertise, she would still take as much time as she or I needed, asked and answered as many questions as needed and if she couldn't help me, she would refer me to somebody who could. Sandra is extremely knowledgeable, professional and knows how to get the job done. I highly recommend Sandra.

-5.0 stars - Posted by Nikki - May 8, 2012

Best lawyer ever!!

Sandra has been a great friend as well as my attorney. She has seen me through numerous legal incidents. She is tenacious in battling for her clients with great charm and dignity and always has your best interests in mind.

-5.0 stars - Posted by Ann - April 22, 2012

S. Worthington Helped me to get my life back

I was injured during a work injury. Sandra was there for me. She even helped when the employer was giving me trouble. First and best lawyer experience.

-5.0 stars - Posted by Marcus - May 8, 2012

Up front direct and no surprises

We have used Sandra many times as hiring, but also to bounce things off her head for advice and direction. She has always guided us in the right direction without expecting anything in return. We have recommended her to many other people and if she couldn't help them she would always direct them to the right kind of attorney.

-5.0 stars - Posted by Judy - May 17, 2011

Smart

I've known Sandy for over 20 years and anytime I had a legal question she has been more than willing to help. We had a need for council about 3 years ago and she came up with all the reasons necessary to come in with a positive conclusion and she won the case. It was against a large corporation, too!

-5.0 stars - Posted by anonymous - January 24, 2011

What if you Need Your Questions Answered NOW?

While I hope this book has been of help to you in understanding brain injuries and how a claim might proceed if a brain injury has resulted from someone's negligence, you may have pressing questions that require an immediate answer. If the insurance company is pressing you for a statement on the phone or has shown up at your door, you need legal help immediately. Remember that a personal injury lawyer with experience in brain injury cases will not charge you for a phone consultation so there is no reason not to call to discuss your case. Certainly, if you wish to reach me to talk about your case, I am available at my office or outside of work hours in an emergency. And, if you are at the point in your journey where you need to hire an attorney, I would be honored to consult with you or your family member. Feel free to call me at my office at 215-576-5150 or contact me through my website at www.WorthingtonLawGroup.com. I've been at that number for 34 years and I will be there if you need me. My office has a 24 hour human answering the phone so unless you are calling on Sunday night or a major holiday you will be greeted by a friendly helpful staff member and connected with me in short order.

Remember that lawyers who appear on TV ads, the yellow pages or the internet with slogans like "100 years of combined experience", "Best lawyer for your case" (completely unethical to say in PA), or "Former Prosecutor" (that would be great if you had been accused of a crime, but this is a brain injury case!), Former State Senator (how does this help him understand brain injuries or personal injury cases? It does not!) --none of these is the best lawyer for your case. The bottom line is you need a highly experienced personal injury lawyer with a depth of knowledge in the area of brain injury who will work tirelessly to get the best possible results for you in a terrible situation. You need experience, knowledge and compassion, plus personal attention to the myriad problems which arise when someone has suffered a brain injury. Choose wisely!

RESOURCES AND SOURCES

Mayo Clinic (www.MayoClinic.org)

Center for Neuro Science and Regenerative Medicine (www.CNRMStudies.org)

Psychiatric Times (www.PsychiatricTimes.com)

National Center for Biotechnology Information (www.ncbi.nlm.nih.gov/)

Journal of Neurosurgery (thejns.org)

Brain Injury Association of America (BIAA) (www.biausa.org)

Make the Connection (maketheconnection.net)

Magee Rehab-Brain Injury Program at Magee Rehabilitation Hospital (PA) (www.mageerehab.org)

Web MD (www.WebMD.com)

American Psychiatric Association (www.psychiatry.org)

IF YOU WOULD LIKE TO READ MORE PLEASE CONTACT US BY PHONE

(215-576-5150)

OR BY EMAIL

(SBW@WORTHINGTONLAWGROUP.COM)

Made in the USA
Monee, IL
04 November 2026

67383610R00036